This book is presented to:

_____

From:

_____

Date:

_____

Tell Me About God
by Karen Henley

Requests for information may be addressed to:

The children's book imprint of Strang Communications Company
600 Rinehart Rd., Lake Mary, FL 32746
www.charismakids.com

Children's Editor: Gwen Ellis
Copyeditor: Jevon Oakman Bolden
Design Director: Mark Poulalion
Designed by Joe De Leon

Library of Congress Control Number 2004115570
International Standard Book Number 1-59185-616-7

05 06 07 08 09 — 9 8 7 6 5 4 3 2 1
Printed in China

Tell Me About

God

by Karyn Henley
Illustrated by David L. Erickson

Charisma
KIDS
A STRANG COMPANY

Tell me. Tell me. Tell me about God. God is the Maker. When He said, "Light!", sparkling brightness showered the heavens. The sky spread out deep and wide like a high tent. God Himself wears light like clothes wrapped around Him. Darkness looks like only a blanket to Him. He never sleeps.

When God said, "Sun! Moon! Stars!", they scattered themselves across the dark sky. The sun glowed fiery hot. The moon poured out its silver beams. Stars winked and blinked as God called each one by its name.

Tell me. Tell me. Tell me about God.
He is the powerful One. When
He said, "Sea!", waves sloshed and
splashed and sprayed. God tells
oceans and rivers where to stay, and
they obey Him. When waves roar
and rush and gush, God makes them
settle down again.

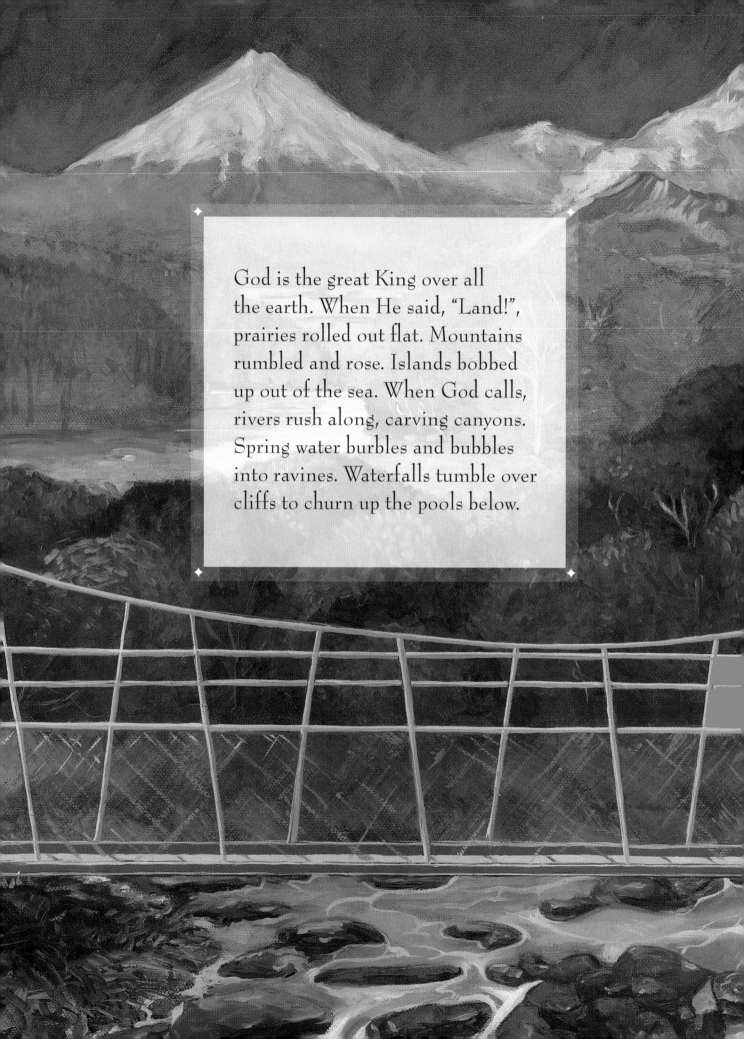

God is the great King over all the earth. When He said, "Land!", prairies rolled out flat. Mountains rumbled and rose. Islands bobbed up out of the sea. When God calls, rivers rush along, carving canyons. Spring water burbles and bubbles into ravines. Waterfalls tumble over cliffs to churn up the pools below.

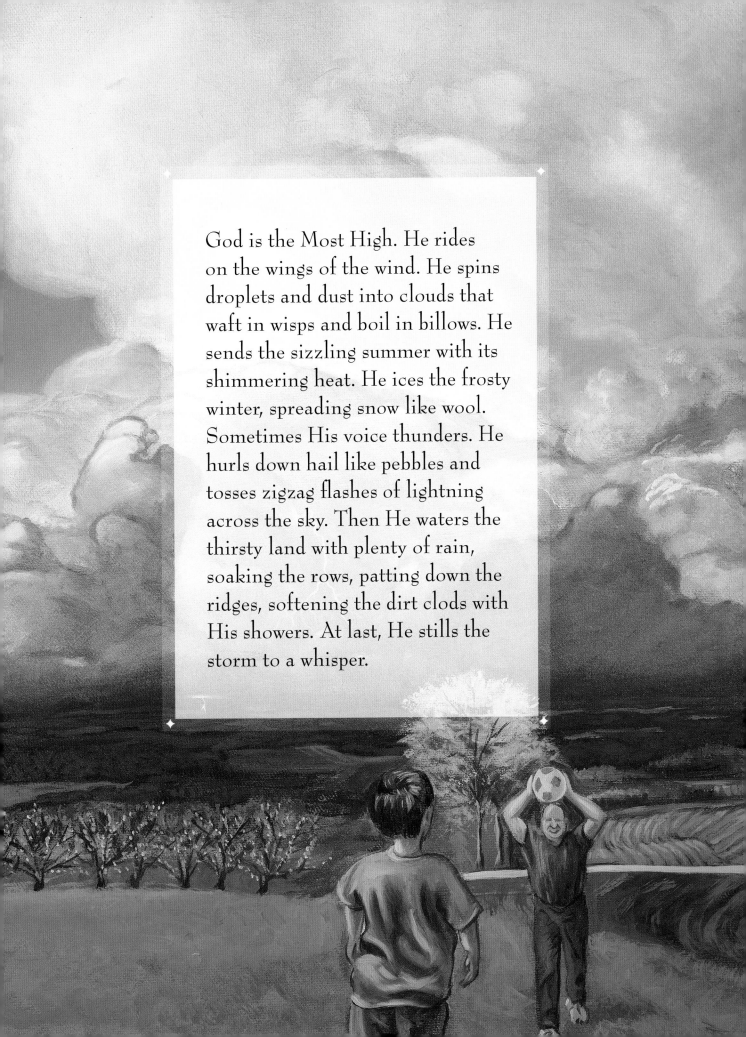

God is the Most High. He rides on the wings of the wind. He spins droplets and dust into clouds that waft in wisps and boil in billows. He sends the sizzling summer with its shimmering heat. He ices the frosty winter, spreading snow like wool. Sometimes His voice thunders. He hurls down hail like pebbles and tosses zigzag flashes of lightning across the sky. Then He waters the thirsty land with plenty of rain, soaking the rows, patting down the ridges, softening the dirt clods with His showers. At last, He stills the storm to a whisper.

Tell me. Tell me. Tell me about God.
He is the Lord of lords. When He
said, "Animals!", they came—furry,
feathery, scaly, leathery. They creep
and climb, leap and lumber, flit
and fly, swim and swagger. They all
belong to God. He owns the wild
ones of the forest and the tame ones
on the hills. He knows every bird in
the mountains.

God is good. When He said, "Plants!", trees stretched their branches, flowers unfurled petals of every color, grasses sprouted, vines curved and curled. God made the plants as food for the animals—wild and tame. And on His earth, He grows flavorful crops for people to eat. He tops off each year with a bountiful harvest of food.

Tell me. Tell me. Tell me about God. God is love. When He said, "People!", He formed a man, and He made a woman. God walked with them and talked with them and loved them. God's hands made even me. He created me from the inside out and saw my body when I was being made. God knit me together inside my mother.

He knows what I do and how I do it. He knows when I sit down and when I get up. He knows when I go out and when I come in. He knows what I think and what I am going to say. God hears my voice. He will never stop loving me.

So, listen, all you angels. Listen sun and moon and stars. Listen mountains and oceans, clouds and wind, trees and flowers, and all you animals. Listen kings and princes, boys and girls. Sing your love to God. Show how great He is. Let everything praise God, because He is the Maker, the powerful One, the great King, the Most High, the Lord of lords. God is good. God is love. I will sing to Him all my life.

Tell you about God?
Ah! Yes!
He's the One who makes me smile.

For parents who want to tell their children about God

Just who is this God who made everything we know? Can any of us parents, let alone our children, truly understand Him? And does He know about little children? Does He care about them?

Yes, yes, and yes, to all the questions above. The awesome God made the sun, moon, and stars. He made the sky and the seas and all the living birds and fish in them. He made the earth and filled it with glorious creatures.

God is good, and God is love. He rides upon the wings of the wind, and He waters the thirsty earth. He made us from the dust of the earth and then tucked within us a bit of His own image. He loved us from the very moment He created us. Afterward God stayed close by—so close that He knows when we rise up and when we lie down and when we go out and when we come in. What He has done for us is truly amazing!

If you, as a parent, have not yet captured the wonder of the God who loves you, read this book over a few times before sharing it with your children. Spend some time thinking about all God has done for you. Then when your children ask you about God, you will be able to tell them how awe-inspiring God is and how complete His love is.

And you'll be able to say with the author:

"Tell you about God?
Ah! Yes!
He's the One who makes me smile."